2/06

**THREE RIVERS
PUBLIC LIBRARY DISTRICT**
www.three-rivers-library.org
Channahon, IL 60410
815-467-6200

TOURING BIKES

MOTORCYCLE MANIA

David and Patricia Armentrout

Rourke
Publishing LLC
Vero Beach, Florida 32964

www.rourkepublishing.com

PHOTO CREDITS: Cover, pp. 5, 22 ©Suzuki; title page, pp. 8 ©PIR; pp. 6, 9, 14, 19, 21 ©Honda; pp. 4 ©Allyson; pp. 20 © Noel Clark; pp. 10, 11, 13, 15, 17 ©thedigitalrose.com

Title page: *Big, comfortable touring bikes are roomy enough for two.*

Editor: Frank Sloan

Cover and page design by Nicola Stratford

Library of Congress Cataloging-in-Publication Data

Armentrout, David, 1962-
  Touring bikes / David and Patricia Armentrout.
      p. cm. -- (Motorcycle mania)
  Summary: "Climb aboard! Imagine cruising the countryside on a big, comfortable touring bike, rocketing down a strip on a drag bike, or gripping the ice in an extreme speedway race! If these excite you, then you are a motorcycle fan" "[summary]"--Provided by publisher.
  Includes index.
  ISBN 1-59515-457-4 (hardcover)
  1. Motorcycles. 2. Motorcycle touring. 3. Motorcycling. I. Armentrout, Patricia, 1960- II. Title. III. Series.

TL440.A7436 2006
629.28'475--dc22

                              2005013576

Printed in the USA

CG/CG

Rourke Publishing
1-800-394-7055
www.rourkepublishing.com
sales@rourkepublishing.com
Post Office Box 3328, Vero Beach, FL 32964

TABLE OF CONTENTS

A motorcycle rider wants a bike that looks cool. But it is more important for riders to have bikes that perform well and fit their size and riding style. Fortunately, it's easier than ever to find a high-performance bike in a variety of styles and sizes.

Riders personalize their bikes with accessories that fit their traveling needs.

It is important to learn to ride safely on a bike that fits your size.

TOURING BIKES

A lot of attention is paid to motorcycle racers and the specialized bikes they ride. But racers are in the **minority**. Most motorbike owners ride around town or simply enjoy a cruise on a Sunday afternoon. Then there's the rider who spends a lot of time touring on his or her bike. Touring bikes are built for long-distance riding.

Bikers ride with their lights on to give them greater visibility.

Almost any motorcycle can be a touring bike, as long as it meets the needs of the rider. Basically, a touring bike should be reliable, comfortable, have storage space, and, of course, be fun to ride.

Cruisers are great for short rides or overnight trips.

A Honda touring bike on the production line

Big, heavy touring bikes give a smooth ride and absorb bumps along the way.

Many custom **cruisers** position the rider's feet out in front and their hands at shoulder height. While this position is fine for shorter rides, it's not comfortable for long distances.

RELIABILITY

Reliability doesn't mean you need a brand new bike. It means you need a bike that can go from one place to another without breaking down. Regular maintenance is the key. Before touring, riders inspect the tires, change the oil, check the battery, and tighten anything that is fastened on.

Bikers take pride in their bikes and constantly keep their machines in tip-top shape.

COMFORT

A touring bike must be comfortable enough for a day-long ride, even for a passenger. Riding style goes hand in hand with comfort. A **dresser** or a **sport-touring** bike keeps a rider in an upright position. This is great for touring. An upright seating position allows riders to stand on the foot pegs and adjust their body position.

Sportbikes are not considered touring bikes, but many riders tour on them. The trouble is, at slow speeds the weight of the rider is carried by the wrists and shoulders. This makes a long ride exhausting.

Bikers travel across the country to attend motorcycle rallies.

One thing that can really tire out a long-distance rider is windblast. Good touring bikes have windshields and body panels, called **fairings**. Fairings are mounted on the front to protect the rider. The size and shape of the fairings depend on the bike.

A sport-touring bike is smaller and sleeker-looking than a full dresser.

A young passenger has a comfortable seat to ride on.

STORAGE

When riders hit the road for a long-distance trip, they must have storage space. Some bikes come with hard luggage mounted on the rear. Bikes without luggage can be made tour-ready by attaching soft luggage with bungee hooks.

Cargo trailers towed behind a bike are for serious travelers. They're great for riders who love to camp and need to haul a lot of supplies and equipment.

The owner of this ride surely likes to be noticed!

FUEL RANGE

Motorcycles have small gas tanks, so planning fuel stops is a must. Big bikes tend to have larger tanks than smaller bikes, but they burn fuel faster. Riders need to know their bike's fuel range.

Tank size x mileage = fuel range
For example, a bike with a 4-gallon (15-liter) tank that gets 35 miles (56 kilometers) per gallon can travel 140 miles (225 kilometers) before needing to refuel. Fuel range can vary, though, depending on speed, load weight, and road conditions.

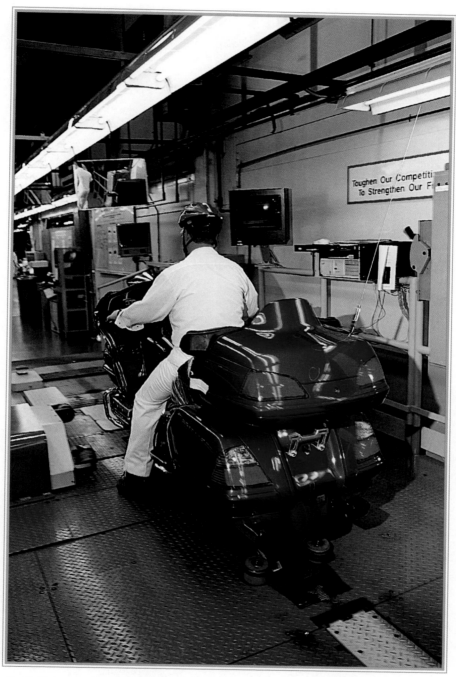

A full-size touring bike passes safety and mechanical inspections before reaching the showroom floor.

A PERSONAL CHOICE

The perfect touring bike is a personal choice. That's why there are so many styles to choose from. Major bike manufacturers like Harley-Davidson, BMW, and Honda all make touring bikes.

Riders have different wants and needs, but they all have one thing in common—they love the adventure of cruising the open road.

Three-wheeled bikes are called trikes. They give riders the advantage of not having to put their feet down at each stop.

The instrument panel on a Honda Goldwing touring bike

A cruiser is built for touring in style with factory leather luggage and matching seats and backrest.

GLOSSARY

cruisers (KRU zurz) — typically heavy, twin-engined, low-riding motorcycles that do not handle well at high speeds or on turns

dresser (DRESS ur) — a term that describes a motorcycle set up for long-distance touring

fairings (FAIR ingz) — devices such as windshields and body panels that are mounted on the front of a motorcycle to protect the rider from windblast

minority (my NOR uh tee) — something in a small number

sportbikes (SPORT BIKES) — light, fast, high performance street-legal motorcycles that handle well at high speeds and on curves

sport-touring (SPORT TOOR ing) — a middle-weight sportbike with some comforts for touring

INDEX

FURTHER READING

Gibbs, Lynne. *Mega Book of Motorcycles*. Chrysalis Education, 2003

Hill, Lee Sullivan. *Motorcycles*. Lerner, 2004

WEBSITES TO VISIT

American Motorcyclist Association
   ama-cycle.org
Canadian Motorcycle Association
   www.canmocycle.ca/

ABOUT THE AUTHORS

David and Patricia Armentrout specialize in writing nonfiction books for young readers. They have had several books published for primary school reading. The Armentrouts live in Cincinnati, Ohio, with their two children.